SOUND *Artistry*
INTERMEDIATE METHOD
for HORN IN F
PETER BOONSHAFT & CHRIS BERNOTAS

in collaboration with
DR. MARGARET TUNG

Thank you for making *Sound Artistry Intermediate Method for Horn in F* a part of your continued development as a musician. This book will help you progress toward becoming a more able and independent musician, focusing on both your technical and musical abilities. It offers material ranging from intermediate to advanced, making it valuable for musicians at various experience levels.

The many instrument-specific exercises in this book will help to support your personal improvement of techniques on your instrument, focusing on skills that may not always be addressed in an ensemble or in other repertoire. You will notice there are many performance and technique suggestions throughout the book. This wonderful advice has been provided by our renowned collaborative partners, as well as the many specialist teachers we worked with to create this book.

Sound Artistry Intermediate Method for Horn in F is organized into lessons that can be followed sequentially. As you progress through each lesson, it is a good idea to go back to previous lessons to reinforce concepts and skills, or just to enjoy performing the music. Exercises include Long Tones, Flexibility, Major and Minor Scales (all forms), Scale Studies, Arpeggio Studies, Chromatic Studies, Etudes, and Duets, as well as exercises that are focused on skills that are particular to your instrument. You will notice that many studies are clearly marked with dynamics, articulations, style, and tempo for you to practice those aspects of performance. Other studies are intentionally left for you to determine those aspects of your musical interpretation and performance. This book progresses through various meters and every key. Once a key has been introduced, previous keys are interspersed throughout for reinforcement and variety. In the back of this book you will also find expanded-range scale pages and a detailed fingering chart.

We wish you all the best as you continue to develop your musicianship, technique, and artistry!

~ Peter Boonshaft and Chris Bernotas

Dr. Margaret Tung is Associate Professor of Horn at the University of Cincinnati College—Conservatory of Music. She has performed with the Chicago Symphony Orchestra, Zurich Opera Orchestra, Cincinnati Symphony, and Baltimore Symphony, to name a few. During the summer, she serves on the faculty of the Bay View Wind Institute and Interlochen Center for the Arts. Dr. Tung is an active member of the International Horn Society and serves on the Advisory Council.

alfred.com

Copyright © 2023 by Alfred Music
All rights reserved. Printed in USA.

ISBN-10: 1-4706-6657-X
ISBN-13: 978-1-4706-6657-6

Instrument photos provided courtesy of Jupiter Band Instruments/KHS America

Lesson 1

DAILY ROUTINE

Start each day with a Long Tone, Flexibility, and Tonguing exercise. This routine will vary from lesson to lesson as new exercises are introduced. Always start your day by trying to achieve your best sound.

1   **LONG TONES**—*For long tones, always strive for a beautiful, consistent sound.*

2   **LONG TONES: CHROMATIC**

3   **FLEXIBILITY**—*Flexibility exercises (or lip-slur exercises) throughout this book should be played on the F side of the horn. Use your air to navigate from note to note.*

4   **C MAJOR SCALE AND ARPEGGIO**—*Be sure to play the quarter-note triplets evenly.*

5   **C MAJOR SCALE STUDY**

6   **ARPEGGIO STUDY**—*Be aware of the changing slur patterns in this study.*

7 **ETUDE**—*Play all etudes slowly with a steady tempo and good tone quality before speeding up. Always keep a good tone in mind and perform with musicality.*

8 **ETUDE**—*Play the sixteenth notes lightly in this etude.*

9 **ETUDE**—*Practice this etude with two-bar phrases and then four-bar phrases.*

10 **DUET**

4

Lesson 2

11 **LONG TONES**

Slowly ♩ = 60

Play the Flexibility study from Lesson 1 before playing exercise 12.

12 **A MINOR SCALE**

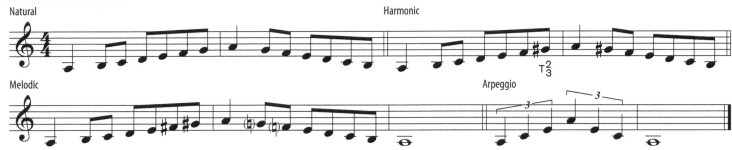

13 **A MINOR SCALE STUDY**

14 **ETUDE**

Moderately ♩ = 72

15 **ETUDE**

Pensively ♩ = 60

16 CHROMATIC SCALE

17 CHROMATIC SCALE ETUDE

Moderately ♩ = 88

18 ETUDE —*Practice this etude slowly at first and gradually increase the speed.*

Lightly ♪ = 120

19 ETUDE—*After playing this etude as written, create or improvise a new ending for the last two measures.*

Moderately ♩ = 100

Lesson 3

20 **LONG TONES**—*Remember to always have proper posture, embouchure, and hand position to promote performing with a beautiful tone.*

21 **FLEXIBILITY**

22 **F MAJOR SCALE AND ARPEGGIO**—*For all scale exercises that are written in octaves, practice each octave separately and then as a two octave scale and arpeggio. Sing or hum these notes before playing them. Internalizing the pitch will help develop your aural skills.*

23 **F MAJOR SCALE STUDY**

24 **ETUDE**—*Play dotted eighth-sixteenth figures in a crisp manner.*

25 **ARPEGGIO STUDY**—*Match the pitch of the first and last note of each measure.*

26 **ETUDE**

27 **DUET**

Lesson 4

Pick a Long Tone, Flexibility, and Tonguing Study/Etude from Lessons 1–3 as your Daily Routine.

28 D MINOR SCALE

29 D MINOR SCALE STUDY

30 ETUDE

31 ETUDE—*Strive for an even tempo and always use a metronome.*

32 **DUET**—*Work towards matching each of the musical elements in this duet for a unified performance.*

33 **ETUDE**—*Play this etude with an eighth-note pulse until the rhythm is accurate. Then, transition to the dotted-quarter-note pulse.*

Lesson 5

Pick a Long Tone, Flexibility, and Tonguing Study/Etude from Lessons 1–4 as your Daily Routine.

34 ETUDE

35 ETUDE

36 ETUDE—*Practice this etude at a slower tempo before speeding up. Always strive for a focused and consistent tone.*

37 **ETUDE**

Stately ♩ = 98

38 **DUET**

Maestoso ♩ = 72

39 **ETUDE**

Cantabile ♩ = 72

Lesson 6

Pick a Long Tone study from a previous lesson before playing exercise 40.

40 FLEXIBILITY

41 G MAJOR SCALE AND ARPEGGIO

42 G MAJOR SCALE STUDY—*Using manuscript paper, or notation software, compose a new scale study that you think is even more challenging.*

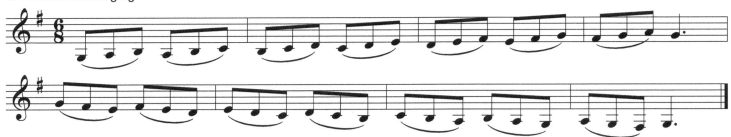

43 RANGE EXTENSION—*When playing in the high register move your air much faster, use the vowel "eee" to encourage the tongue to raise in the oral cavity, and keep a flat chin with firm corners.*

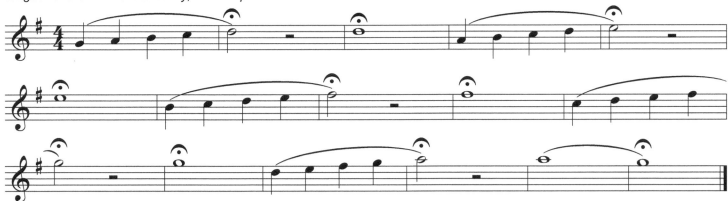

44 BASS CLEF—*Horn has a wide range and will sometimes have notes written in bass clef. The second half of this exercise (which is written in bass clef) will sound one octave below the first half. When playing in the low register, use slower air but also a large amount of air. Your jaw should be forward and down and you should articulate notes lower on the top teeth. Have a firm anchor on the bottom lip and keep the corners firm.*

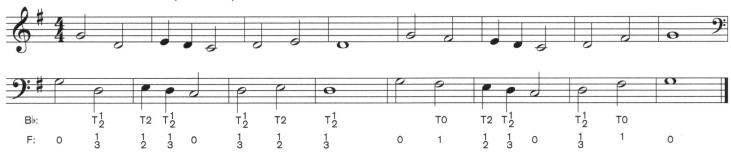

45 **INTERVAL STUDY**—*Once you are comfortable with this as written, practice it an octave higher. Play quarter notes full value, giving special attention to the lower notes. This exercise can also be played with varying articulations like staccato and marcato.*

46 **ETUDE**

Andantino ♩ = 80

47 **ETUDE**—*Switching between the F and B♭ side of the horn can help produce smoother slurs in the middle register in certain circumstances. Notice the fingering marked in the second to last measure. Practice this etude with two-bar phrases and then four-bar phrases.*

Dolce ♩ = 80

48 **ETUDE**

Moderately ♩ = 112

Lesson 7

Pick a Long Tone study from a previous lesson before playing exercise 49.

49 FLEXIBILITY

50 E MINOR SCALE

51 E MINOR SCALE STUDY

52 ETUDE

53 RANGE EXTENSION—*Note the change of clef in measure 9.*

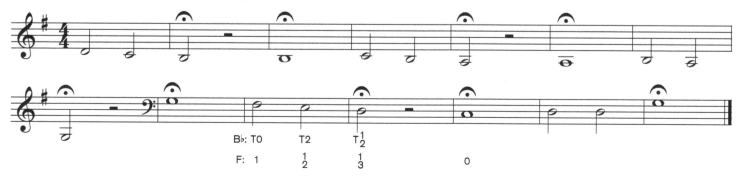

54 ETUDE—*Make sure the strong beats are on 1 and 3, and not on the quarter notes on 2 and 4.*

55 ETUDE—*After successfully playing this etude, seek guidance from a teacher for ways you can refine your performance.*

56 ETUDE

Lesson 8

Pick a Long Tone study from a previous lesson before playing exercise 57.

57 FLEXIBILITY

58 Bb MAJOR SCALE AND ARPEGGIO

59 Bb MAJOR SCALE STUDY

60 ETUDE—*If this exercise is not rhythmically even at the dotted-quarter-note pulse, try setting your metronome to the eighth-note pulse of ♪ = 180.*

61 ETUDE—*Be creative with the musicality of this etude by altering and adding your own dynamic markings.*

62 DUET

63 G MINOR SCALE

64 G MINOR SCALE STUDY—*Play the sixteenth notes for their full value. Try not to clip them, especially in the second to last bar. Think of the sixteenth notes as having a tenuto, it keeps the air moving through the technique.*

65 ETUDE

Lesson 9

Pick a Long Tone, Flexibility, and Tonguing Study/Etude from a previous lesson before playing this lesson.

GRACE NOTES are ornaments that are performed before the beat or on the beat, depending on the musical time period, style, context, and notation. The last example below shows how unslashed grace notes would be performed in the Classical period. Listen to music from various historical periods and notice the different approaches to the performance of grace notes.

Most often performed before the beat | Classical period, no slash. On the beat (in time).

66 GRACE NOTES—*Play these grace notes just before the main note.*

67 ETUDE

68 ETUDE—*An appoggiatura is a grace note without a slash that is played on the beat. In this exercise, measures 1 and 5, as well as measures 3 and 7, would be played the same.*

69 ETUDE

70 ETUDE

71 **ETUDE**

72 **ETUDE**—*Record your performance of this etude. Recognize the personal musical growth you have made from when you sight-read the piece. Think about the technical and musical ways your performance has improved. Do you hear a difference?*

73 **ETUDE**—*Watch for the accidentals. Practice one measure at a time.*

Lesson 10

74 **LONG TONES**

75 **FLEXIBILITY**

76 **ETUDE**

77 **ETUDE**

78 CHROMATIC SCALE—*Practice this exercise both tongued and slurred. Exaggerate firmly pressing down the valves to keep the rhythm even.*

79 CHROMATIC RANGE—*Be sure to maintain good air support throughout the exercise. Practice this exercise both slurred and tongued.*

80 MAJOR SCALE RANGE—*Keep your body relaxed when playing in the upper register. Practice this exercise both slurred and tongued.*

81 DUET

Andante ♩ = 108

Lesson 11

Pick a Long Tone study from a previous lesson before playing exercise 82.

82 FLEXIBILITY—*Remember that constant air support is key for exercises like this.*

83 D MAJOR SCALE AND ARPEGGIO

84 D MAJOR SCALE STUDY

Moderately ♩ = 120

85 ETUDE

Adagio ♩ = 60

86 ETUDE

Allegro ♩ = 90

mf sempre staccato

continued on next page

87 **ETUDE**

88 **ETUDE**—*After performing this etude, discuss the various elements of the musical work with a peer or teacher.*

89 **ETUDE**

Lesson 12

Pick a Long Tone study from a previous lesson before playing exercise 90.

90 FLEXIBILITY

91 B MINOR SCALE

92 B MINOR SCALE STUDY

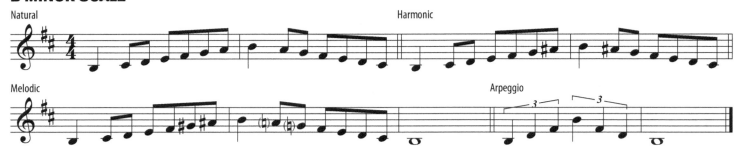

93 B MINOR SCALE STUDY

94 DUET

A **TRILL** is an ornament that is performed by alternating rapidly between the written note and the next diatonic note above. Sometimes you will see a natural, sharp, or flat sign with a trill, which means to alternate between the written note and the next altered note. Always check the key signature.

On horn, valves are used for half-step trills and lip trills are used for whole-step trills.

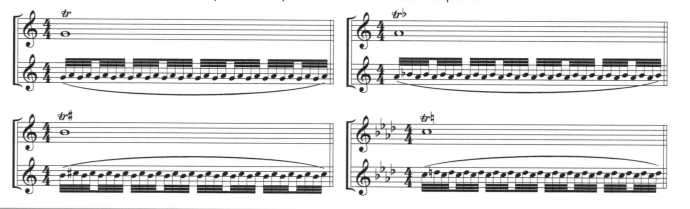

95 **TRILLS**—*Use your metronome to ensure an even and consistent rhythm. This trill exercise uses the lip trill technique. Use the fingering $\frac{1}{3}$ to practice this skill.*

96 **TRILLS**—*Practice this exercise to ensure your trills are played evenly. Once you are comfortable with this exercise as written, try playing it in cut time (♩=160).*

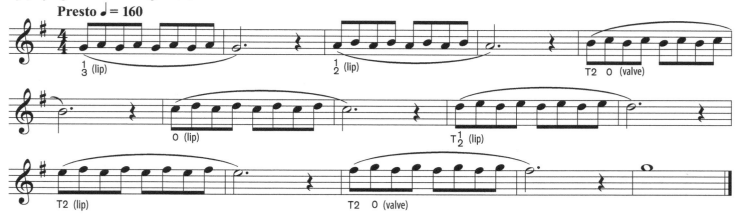

97 **TRILLS**—*Practice measures 1–5 at a slow tempo to reinforce muscle memory, gradually increasing the tempo. This exercise will help ensure that your trills are played evenly.*

98 **ETUDE**—*Depending on the style or historical context, a trill may start with an upper neighbor as shown here. Practice these trills with and without the upper neighbor. Also, grace notes are often used at the end of a trill. This ornament is also known as a nachschläge.*

Lesson 13

Pick a Long Tone study from a previous lesson before playing exercise 99.

99 FLEXIBILITY

100 E♭ MAJOR SCALE AND ARPEGGIO

101 E♭ MAJOR SCALE STUDY

Andante ♩ = 88

102 ETUDE

Andantino ♩ = 90

103 ETUDE

Allegretto ♩. = 80

104 **DUET**

28

Lesson 14

105 LONG TONES—*Focus on a consistent tone when changing notes. Always strive for a beautiful tone.*

106 FLEXIBILITY

107 C MINOR SCALE

108 C MINOR SCALE STUDY

109 ETUDE

110 **DUET**

111 **ETUDE**

112 **DUET**—*While playing duets, both performers must listen critically to evaluate and adjust intonation.*

Lesson 15

Pick a Long Tone study from a previous lesson before playing exercise 113.

113 FLEXIBILITY

114 A MAJOR SCALE AND ARPEGGIO

115 A MAJOR SCALE STUDY

116 ETUDE—*Bring out the stylistic differences between notes marked with slurs, staccatos, and accents. Be sure the dotted-eighth notes and sixteenth notes do not sound like triplets.*

117 ETUDE—*Work for a singing style, ensuring all notes are played for their full value.*

118 **LONG TONES**—*Add a crescendo and decrescendo as you hold each note for at least eight counts. Drop your jaw slightly as you descend to help with the low register.*

119 **F♯ MINOR SCALE**

120 **F♯ MINOR SCALE STUDY**—*Focus on having an even tone throughout. The tone color should stay consistent.*

121 **ETUDE**

Lesson 16

Pick a Long Tone, Flexibility, and Tonguing Study/Etude from previous lessons before playing exercise 122.

122 **DUET**—*When playing ♪♩, remember to think of a sixteenth-note subdivision.*

123 **ETUDE**—*Bring out the accents in this etude.*

124 DUET—*What musical elements in this duet make it engaging? How does the form contribute to the musical work?*

125 ETUDE

Lesson 17

Pick a Long Tone study from a previous lesson before playing exercise 126.

126 FLEXIBILITY

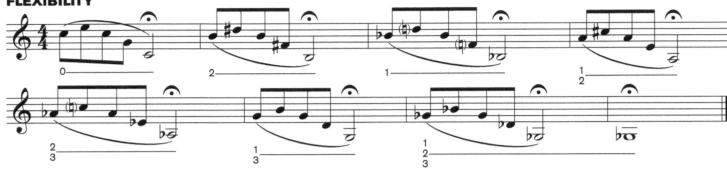

127 Ab MAJOR SCALE AND ARPEGGIO

A **TURN** or **GRUPPETTO** is an ornament that involves playing the written note, followed by the note above it, returning to the original note, then playing the note below it, and finally ending on the original note.

128 Ab MAJOR SCALE STUDY

129 Ab MAJOR SCALE STUDY

130 ETUDE—*Practice this etude slowly, paying careful attention to the key, before playing at a faster speed.*

continued on next page

131 **F MINOR SCALE**

Natural   Harmonic

Melodic   Arpeggio

132 **F MINOR SCALE STUDY**

Allegro ♩ = 132

mf

133 **ETUDE**

Adagio ♩ = 72

mf   *p*

mf

f

mp

Lesson 18

134 LONG TONES—*Match the tone colors of each octave. The lower note should be just as resonant as the upper octave.*

Slowly ♩= 60

135 FLEXIBILITY

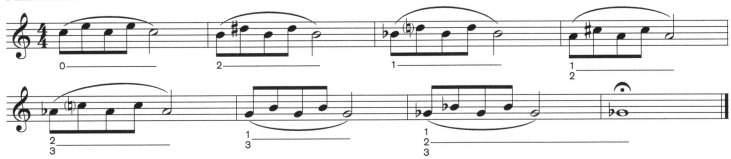

136 E MAJOR SCALE AND ARPEGGIO

137 E MAJOR SCALE STUDY

Moderately ♩= 100

138 ETUDE

Andante ♩= 108

139 ETUDE

Adagio ♩.= 60

37

140 C# MINOR SCALES

Natural

Harmonic

Melodic

Arpeggio

141 C# MINOR SCALE STUDY

Moderato ♩ = 108

mf

142 ETUDE

Allegro ♩ = 120

mf

143 DUET

Adagio ♩ = 66

mf

mf

Lesson 19

Pick a Long Tone study from a previous lesson before playing exercise 144.

144 FLEXIBILITY

STOPPED HORN is a technique in which the player pushes their hand firmly into the bell, creating a muted tone. Stopped horn produces a sound one half step higher than written, which requires the player to transpose the notes one half step lower. The **+** marking indicates that the note should be played stopped.

When this is notated: Use this fingering:

145 STOPPED HORN—*Since the top line of this duet is performed with stopped horn, both lines should sound the same pitches.*

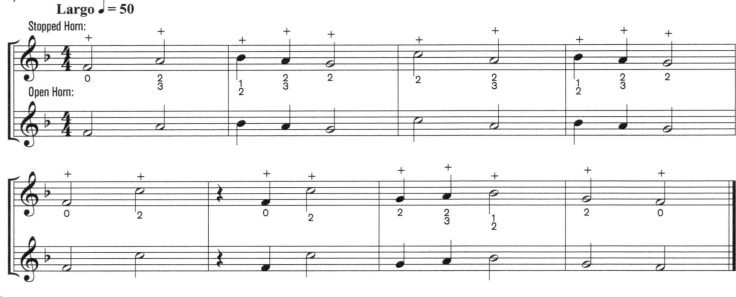

146 ETUDE

147 ETUDE

continued on next page

148 **DUET**

149 **ETUDE**

150 **DUET**—*Use critical listening to improve the performance of all musical elements in this duet.*

Lesson 20

Fast, articulated passages often require the use of a technique called **DOUBLE TONGUING**. Double tonguing is a rapid articulation that alternates using the front/tip of the tongue and back of the tongue. Often, the syllables Tu Ku or Du Gu are used to help understand the tongue placement of this technique.

Tu Ku Tu Ku Tu
Du Gu Du Gu Du

151 **DOUBLE TONGUING EXERCISE**—*For this exercise, practice four Tu articulations, then four Ku articulations, working toward making them sound the same. Then, practice double tonguing by alternating between Tu and Ku, still ensuring they sound the same. Use critical listening and experimentation to match the sound of each syllable. Keep the air moving and the tongue as forward as possible. It can be beneficial to practice saying the multiple tonguing syllables out loud.*

152 **DOUBLE TONGUING EXERCISE**—*As you become comfortable with this technique, increase the tempo and perform these exercises as fast as possible. Apply this pattern to other scales.*

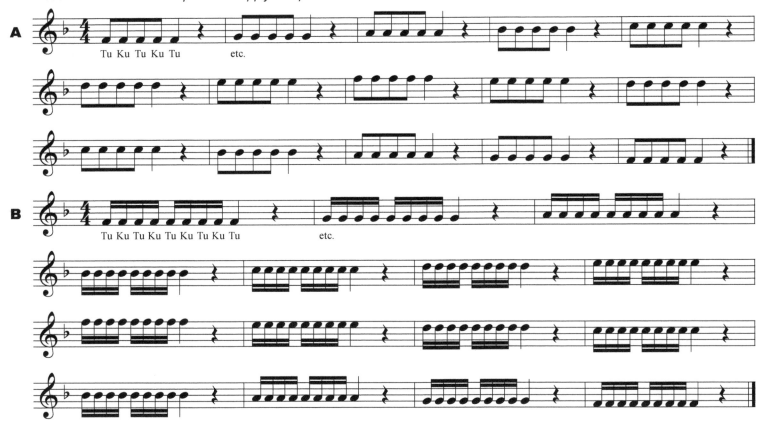

153 **DOUBLE TONGUING EXERCISE**—*Sometimes the syllables Tee Kee are used as well. Experiment to see which syllables work best for you in all ranges of the instrument.*

Fast, articulated passages in three-note groupings often require the use of a technique called **TRIPLE TONGUING**. Triple tonguing is a rapid articulation that alternates using the front/tip of the tongue and back of the tongue. Often, the syllables Tu Tu Ku or Du Du Gu are used to help understand the tongue placement of this technique. Use critical listening and experimentation to match the sound of each syllable.

Tu Tu Ku Tu Tu Ku Tu
Du Du Gu Du Du Gu Du

154 **TRIPLE TONGUING EXCERCISE**

155 **TRIPLE TONGUING EXERCISE**

156 **TRIPLE TONGUING EXERCISE**—*Try playing this triple tonguing scale pattern in other keys.*

157 **ETUDE (FANFARE)**—*Practice this with both single and double tonguing.*

Fanfare ♩ = 120

158 **ETUDE (FANFARE)**—*Practice this with both single and triple tonguing.*

Majestic ♩ = 100

159 **DUET**

Majestic ♩ = 108

Lesson 21

Pick a Long Tone study from a previous lesson before playing exercise 160.

160 FLEXIBILITY

161 D♭ MAJOR SCALE AND ARPEGGIO

162 ETUDE

163 ETUDE

164 B♭ MINOR SCALES

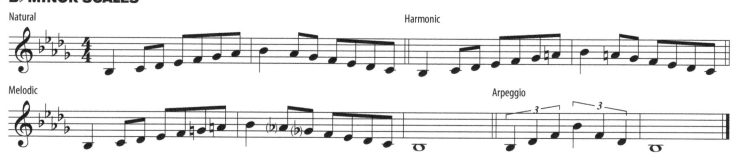

165 ETUDE

Lesson 22

166 LONG TONES

Pick a Flexibility study from a previous lesson before playing exercise 167.

167 B MAJOR SCALE AND ARPEGGIO

168 ETUDE

169 ETUDE

170 A♭ MINOR SCALE *(enharmonic spelling of G♯ minor)*

171 ETUDE

Major Scales

Minor Scales

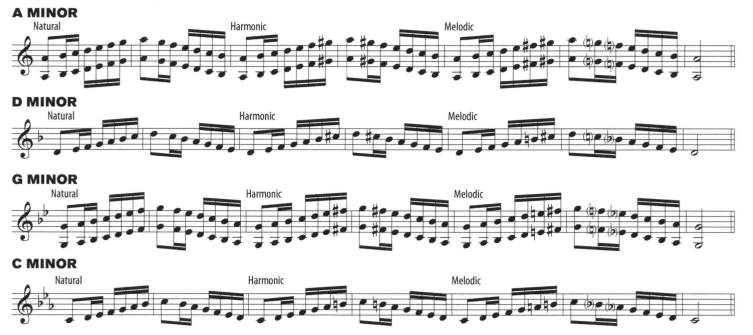

Horn in F Fingering Chart

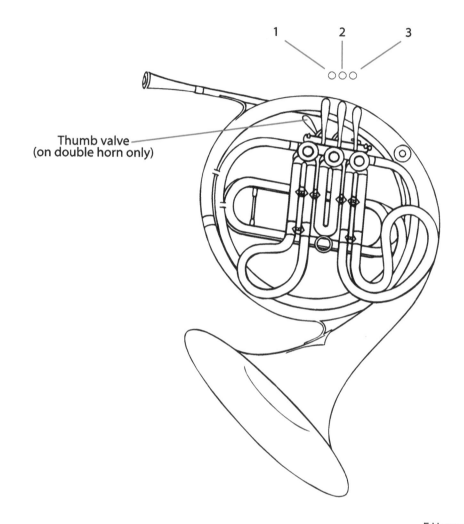

Thumb valve
(on double horn only)

○ = open
● = pressed down

F Horns: Use the upper fingerings.
B♭ Horns: Use the lower fingerings.
The "T" only applies to double horns.

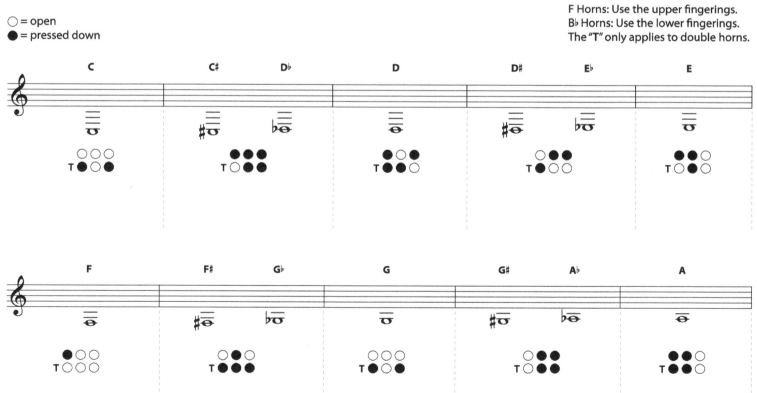

48

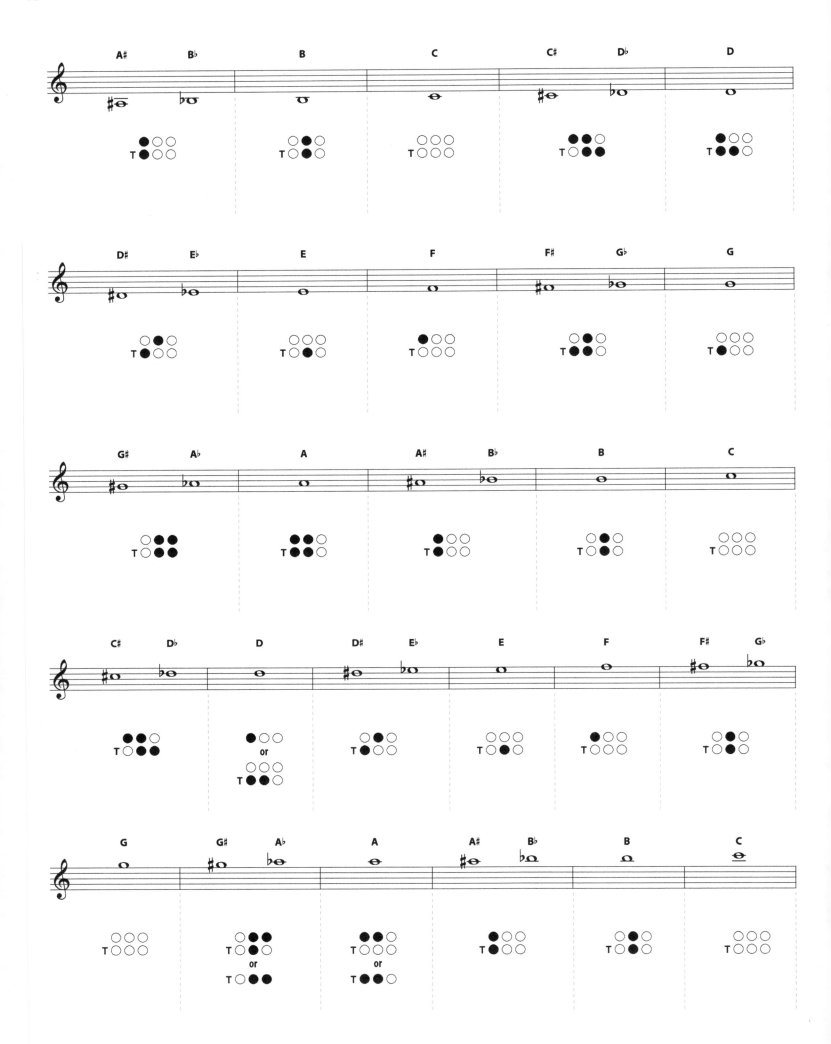